ISLAND LIGHT

ISLAND LIGHT

EUGENE RICHIE

for Helena,

"your luck was in the cards"

with best wishes,

Eugene
4/14/98

Painted Leaf Press
New York City

ACKNOWLEDGMENTS

Grateful acknowledgment is made to the following publications, in which some of these poems first appeared: *Bad Henry*, *The Denver Quarterly*, *Gnosis*, *The Missouri Review*, *Mudfish*, *O-blek*, and *Private: Arts*.

Cover Painting by Jane Freilicher: *Early New York Evening*, 1954

Book design by Brian Brunius and Bill Sullivan

LIBRARY OF CONGRESS CATALOGING-IN-PUBLICATION DATA

Richie, Eugene.
    Island light : poems / Eugene Richie.
        p.   cm.
    ISBN 0-9651558-8-9
    I. Title.
    PS3568.I342I71998
    811'.54--DC21

                                                    97-40859
                                                    CIP

For Joseph and Rosanne

Table of Contents

On the River

The last time we had dinner together,
it was a rainy autumn evening in Manhattan
and the taxi's windshield wipers
refracted the glare of oncoming cars. You said
it was your night to unwind after a long week,
that once recently, in the middle of the day,
you had looked up from your desk and
a wave of anxiety had poured over you.
You suddenly felt that you'd forgotten to call somebody
or that someone was upset with you
for neglecting a friendship.

If this feeling doesn't go away, you will
have to do something about it.
You can't stay up all night wondering what to do
because that won't make it any better. You'll just
have to think it out on your own, slowly but surely.

The lights of cars turn on one by one
along the city street that tapers off
into the twilight sky on the horizon,
and traffic flows naturally
like the stream I saw this afternoon,
bordered by snow in the forest beside the train.

There is a strange similarity
in these two scenes,

like looking into a mirror one day and seeing
the features of my father there
and remembering the way
he used to rub his hands together
before getting into the car
to drive home along the river
or the way the bright dashboard
was reflected outside the window
in the cold night air.

Screen Digest

To breathe this air,
to touch your face,
to hear these birds
singing now outside our open window
is to know you belong to everyday.

For you, anything you want,
I'll do it yesterday.
You come to me with tales to astonish
from the antique auto show
or you disappear without a sound
into the Florida night.

It's always worth it
to spend a few moments of each day with you
trying to outwit one of the evil idiots of the world.

So that's the way it is, is it?
The lobe of your ear,
the end of my tongue,
an old friendlier version
of putting words in my mouth—
and you always come up
with the great ideas. Remember the time we
went to Jones Beach and then
visited the pet mansion?

They told us some people even
buy yachts for their cats.

The Palisades rise up before us
like gates to the gardens
on the western sky. The alluring circle
of the sun is falling now. Whoops!
There it goes.

The Black Pines

A contingency is something that may or may not happen,
when all the black pines are heavy with snow.
You have no control over it, nor does it control you,
but often it's an open book to a future life.

When all the black pines are heavy with snow,
the way to the village leads past the bay,
but often it's an open book to a future life,
through six lanes of cars and a tent of lights.

The way to the village leads past the bay,
beyond a fitness center and a motor inn,
through six lanes of cars and a tent of lights,
to a room and a lamp on a desk near a phone.

Beyond a fitness center and a motor inn,
you turn right after the bridge and head north
to a room and a lamp on a desk near a phone
in our silver palace with its lawn of ice.

You turn right after the bridge and head north.
You have no control over it, nor does it control you.
In our silver palace with its lawn of ice,
a contingency is something that may or may not happen.

In the Rain

The leaf does not fall far
from the branch and the wind that touches it
still touches the wood. You too
leave your fingerprints
on the surface of what others have given you.
When you come up for air,
after a struggle with the water and waves,
that warm body you hold onto is a new world,
breathes just like you do,
is part of you too for a while.

Even now at the table a child
is eating the soft white pulp of a slice of bread,
the grain of the earth, a reward
for vigilance and desire. The knowledge born
in each act, in every generation,
appears in the hum and glow of an evening sunset
or in the bright colors of fruit
stacked in rectangles and pyramids
in the wooden stand on the corner.

Are we alone in this labyrinth,
or are we surrounded by memories
of those who were with us when we reached its center
but who have returned to tell others
how we found our way there
and back again to the sandy beach

where we once waved to a sailor
standing on the prow of the ship
that had brought us to this shore?

This patter at the window is enough for today,
but tomorrow will bring light
and music to help us on our way.

Island Light

She came walking in out of the sunlight
on that warm August afternoon,
but out on the surface of the sea another light
fell endlessly from early morning until dark.

"Once you get your feet on the ground
you'll warm up to it," she said.
"If you don't cash in your chips too early
and head for higher ground."
There were no aftershocks from Saturday's heat wave,
so everyone slept peacefully all night long.
Then the rain began to fall, cooling down
the hot streets, raising waves of mist
into the thick, mild morning air.
That part was all Hollywood.
Even she must have clothes in her dresser drawers
that she never wears.

During the day, the same channel
plays horror movies, and there's one
that shows country-western music videos.
Who is that anyhow, standing
up against the stone fireplace next to a
roaring blaze that is taking the chill off the old lodge?
The comedy hour begins at nine,
but he's not sure he'll be there then.
What was needed was a writer

who could tap nature on the wrist
so as not to lose control of the show, but
what's the use, since the whole
landscape will be changed when he wakes up tomorrow?
He'll take a last look before he turns in for the night
and try to remember the lay of the land.
That way it'll be easier to get going in the morning.

"What a miracle! Let me hear that again,
you want to fly with me to L.A.?" she said.
The sky was an endless shade of red—sunset city!
"The flowers are for you," he said. "Thank you,
for taking that long ride in the desert alone."

And now the curtain of night
has fallen. Summer came back to the city
and it was good, full of that stubborn
American pluck, easy street.

What does he have to be sorry about?
He hasn't lost his mind. Ask Ed. He's been a
brother to him. He'll be a brother to you too.
She was the friend of his cousin or maybe
the cousin of his friend, but
he can't just sit there; he has to follow that car.

In the morning fog she ordered a spring cleaning
of the network news. Your epic, my epic—

a controversy over that white blouse,
so it was all theory, or culture shock.

"You don't mind traipsing all the way over here, do you?"
"I can't wait to get home."
"What's the name of the game that they play?"
"If I knew I wouldn't be asking you.
Still, we need an afternoon in the country
soon, before the warranty on my car expires.
Call before the middle of the week. It's a long
time to wait, and there are other clothes to wear
that neither you nor I have tried on recently,
but we don't have time to think about that now."

Jimmy's Calendar

Kindness consists in loving people
more than they deserve.
~Joseph Joubert

For July, a 1956 blue Cadillac Eldorado,
once someone's necessary object, now an antique,
but how can I recover what is not an object,
though no less necessary? We know how easy it is
to reverse the standard, to ignore the progress
that has been made, once we're on the other side,
but we all slip back into Dimension X now and then.
Sometimes we just have to accept
the incompatibility of systems
and start over from there, remembering
when someone says we can't go there,
that we can and we must.

I've studied the county map and driven through a maze
of country roads. Once I even tried to cross over a pass
to the Interstate only to find ourselves ridge-hopping
in the middle of a downpour, descending
onto the same road going north.
Another time I crossed the Mad River twice
over two different covered bridges
searching for a shorter route to the east and
ended up on the exact same road again going south,
back in the direction from which we had come.

No wonder she wanted us to call her and we did,
but she didn't answer the phone.

I was told there would be days like this,
but not how many. I still haven't figured out
why that circus wagon ended up on top of the evergreen bush
in front of our home last evening. It seemed to have
          something to do
with a magnetic field and an approaching vehicle.
I knew you were in there, and when I went to rescue you
the light of a lamp in the living room
illuminated your exit onto the stone patio.
Years ago, at that time of the day, homeowners
would have been picking up the evening edition
          from their doorsteps,
wondering why they went to work every day
when the office was more like a war zone
than anything resembling work.

It's not just another day, another dollar; it's holding off chaos
at the threshold, a thousand gestures a day to organize
and reorganize in all the possible combinations,
letting as few things as possible slip away.
Check his wallet. Get those wonderful toys.

Gothic Novel

If only I had trusted my instincts,
then I wouldn't be here now, overheating
like an old car in the sun
by the side of the road. Last night
I fell asleep worrying about the dilemma of free will,
whether I do or don't have one.
Tonight I may be thinking about something else,
about what my father meant when he used to say,
"He'll talk your ear off if you let him."

Later, on my walk through the park
I stopped to talk to the woman
who was sitting with a woman and another man.
She was hoping some luck would come to us
from far away, but nobody was able
to lift the veil, though the man on the bench
was quick to say that an ounce of prevention
is worth a pound of cure, but she wasn't listening to him
because she was talking to me,
saying, with the air of trying to clear up
a misunderstanding which had somehow
gotten started earlier in the conversation,
"Oh! the brother, you mean," and finally
the whole thing made sense again.

The scent of her hair lingers in the hall. As he
walks through the open double doors,

there she is, sitting on a bench
next to the water fountain someone was cleaning
with his bare hands only moments ago.
He too is alone on this winter night.
She doesn't know why, but she really likes him
and then their exquisite descent begins
before he can answer her last question
and tears begin to cloud his eyes.

Tonight he has no doubt about how he feels
because every lamp in the room is ablaze,
has been pouring out light endlessly
since he arrived home hours ago to wait for her.
In what solitary corner of the universe was she sitting,
composing an answer to the message he wrote
on the back of a napkin in a coffee shop downtown
under the shadow of a bridge that crosses
a river of moonlight in the luminous night.

In This Diminishing Hour

You can't get at a sunset naming colors.
~James Schuyler, "Hudson Ferry"

As the sound of church bells echoes up and down
this evening river valley, a weight hangs on you
like the pendulous sun on the stormy horizon.

Somewhere beyond it are signposts to point out
directions you could take to reach the heart
of a labyrinth where all the voices converge,

but way back there the train derailed or simply
stopped working and that wrench in the spokes
has caused a relentless fog to cloud the lens

in your usually clear vision of how the world
works, or why the newsboy keeps his appointed
rounds and delivers the paper to your door.

What use is there worrying about it, except
to restore the precise balance, the slender
lines that have somehow crossed in the mind

and are now hotter than ever. You and I
are alone together silently in this room
where flowers burst into light and shadow

while outside the cool leaves of vines
and trees hug the sides of brick
buildings rising just beyond the window ledge.

Perhaps love is the only thing
that can draw you away from the chaos
of hungry mouths waiting over there in repose.

But it's not a question of life on the other side.
Here in this valley rain beats against windowpanes,
spattering them with the mud of a dirty sky.

There is much to be glad about and much to regret.
Caught in the cord around your feet, you may
trip and fall with a splash onto the rain-dark sidewalk.

Yet amends can be made, the whole thing patched up
and sent on its way again down the midnight corridor
toward another day when a new appointment or plan

will turn the mood around to sunlight.

From Pillar to Post

It's that time of evening again. The golden pines
pine now amid the scattered leaves and tall
birch trees. The globe has decked a ridge
behind. Thick fog lies on the hills ahead.

Those huge white letters the size of houses
out there in the woods are turning
into the neon-red words MOTEL and GOLF,
bigger than life, almost real.

It was summer then when all the tangled lines
converged at the familiar hub in the center
of the city where you found the taxi of your dreams,
yellow and black and something like a featherbed.

Don't walk underneath that chandelier
unless you've already returned your lawyer's call.
We could have breakfast soon, but
where is your lost musical score?

We'll find that trail and follow it,
like the row of taillights along the water
in front of those apartment-building windows
hovering on the horizon in the night sky.

The bridge's green triangle of lights
reaches almost to the stars only to fall again

at the foot of the blazing torch that rises and
descends in a column of fire at the river's edge.

It's time for spy versus spy at the astronomer's banquet,
a roar of voices like a storm at sea
—North Road, Near Road, Hollow Road,
Salt Point Turnpike, Jackson Corners Road,

Bullet Hole Road, Nine Partners Road,
Pumpkin Lane, Willow Brook Road,
Willow Lane, Bulls Head Road,
Cold Spring Road, Pudding Street.

Discarded Finery

The full moon's peach is in the key of F:
Every good boy—or girl—deserves favor. So
it's time to count their beads or blessings.

Then why does it always begin like this:
because love is blind even if it can lift them
from rags to riches in the eleventh hour?
Now they've landed in the lap of luxury
like the metallic light that streams down
through the branches of those leafless poplars
which rise above a block of abandoned,
burnt-out buildings, reminding them of the enigma
of their arrival. But that pin-striped suit
he wore to the Beggar's Ball can be preserved,
hauled out for yet another year before it is
returned to storage like the rose she wore
on their first formal date, placed between
the leaves of that illuminated manuscript
someone left in her library long ago.

But this story has a happy ending and
you won't have to hear it again to realize
that she's right about the way
his hair should be parted, that he's right
about the shade of color on her eyelids
under the trembling light of early evening
and about the pure sorcery of the wish he made

one night while re-reading the final chapter
of that book about men and maidens
he bought last January
to remind himself of how ruthless
love can be.

Kingston Bridge

The light gleams for an instant and then it's gone,
Trailing its tails of gold
Over every high window, leaf and branch.
Evening falls softly
Onto the boughs of maple trees,
Hemlocks begin to droop and drowse
Above newly mowed lawns.

Such a long time for such a small time,
But you are not alone in that fleeting hour.
The anxious voices of birds and crickets fill the air
And darker clouds gather on the western horizon
Beneath an aureole of fading light.

Night falls swiftly like unpinned hair
Around a woman's bare shoulders at bedtime.
The faces of those you love appear before you
Like random lights in neighboring windows
That shine with a dull glow,

While the whistle of a train,
Near some station at the water's edge,
Echoes up and down the blue river valley.

Summer Song

I am so close to you at times
that when I walk out the door
to catch a bus or train, it's like I'm
leaving something behind, forgetting
what I should have taken with me.

What do I remember most? How to be true
to what I remember? How not to make it up
if I don't? That time we went go-go dancing
at the Europa? Or that afternoon we were
bound for Babylon, together, inseparable,
side by side for hour after hour, past
the Continental Bakery, the home of Wonder Bread?
Together we've seen novelties, displays,
and much more.
                          If I could never again
see the profile of your face, the crescent
of your left ear, the shape of your right arm,
the shades of your hair;
                          never again
feel your hand's warmth, still clinging to an object
you have just set down;
                          never again
touch the inside of your thigh, the tip of your ear,
the firmness of your back, the line of your eyebrow,
the back of your head,

then I would be one step further away
from paradise on earth.

But the branches keep growing higher and closer
to me every day. I am surrounded by all this
greenness and have only a brief view of the sailboats
in the narrow bay. In your presence, another day
dawns before me, opening out
toward that great body of water
that leads to the glistening horizon
beyond the cloudy curve of the morning sky.

The Luxembourg Gardens

for Joseph

Sunlight bathed the palace
and illuminated the orange-tree leaves
With long sticks children moved the boats in the fountain
The hooves of horses clattered in the trees
You rode in the cart with the other little ones
behind the thirsty little pony
Lemonade and ice cream at the outdoor café
How dark it was in the puppet theater
Intermission and the lights go up
You tested every door for a way out
Only Pierre and I stayed to see Guignol
become the secretary of the prince

Tennis balls whizzed through the summer air
The sounds of children's voices
They are splashing in the wading pool,
water in their eyes
Where are the dry towels?

There on a bench sat Pierre, Rosanne, and I
You brought water in a purple watering can
to bathe your mother's feet
She was a plant ready to bloom,
a flower opening in the sun
Even the newsstand sold shovels, buckets and balls

When Pierre returned from the Bon Marché
with arms full of Roget & Gallet shampoo
and other fragrances,
I found you and mama playing on the lawn
at the foot of a statue of Liberty

American Fresco

May miracles never cease to move you,
as the wind moves the boughs of pines
and the branches of budding trees above the wet bank
beside the northbound railroad tracks.

As the wind moves the boughs of pines
("Please make sure that I'm awake at Broadway.")
beside the northbound railroad tracks,
I will be making announcements.

("Please make sure that I'm awake at Broadway.")
Just ask and your wish shall be granted;
I will be making announcements—
once upon a time, your moment in the sun.

Just ask and your wish shall be granted.
What music have you heard in the rustling pages of the *Times*—
once upon a time, your moment in the sun?
Your fortune in the *Post* says you will always be young.

What music have you heard in the rustling pages of the *Times*
and the branches of budding trees above the wet bank?
Your fortune in the *Post* says you will always be young.
May miracles never cease to move you.

Sea Breezes

With a red sky at morning, sailors take warning,
but a red sky at night is a sailor's delight.
Here I am on the day of departure, seeing things
from the other side again, setting out at dawn

to view the beauty and the tragedy of it all,
and the first thing someone asks me is
"Where are you going, skipper?" So innocence
is beyond irony, but what is before it?

One thing I've learned is that people who live
in glass houses shouldn't throw stones
so it's never too late to make amends
or scatter your garden's weeds to the wind.

It's the way I feel about something
I thought I would never see or hear again,
the flutter of an eyelash, the sound of a kiss, but whose
watch is this anyhow? Mine or a distant uncle's?

On the day before the day before yesterday
(yes, on Saturday! or was it Friday?—at any rate
it wasn't during the day, but at night), I dreamt
about an afternoon at sea beneath a deep blue sky.

So was that the same night I first looked back
with a smile on what before was so serious,

remembering I could have gotten up to leave?
Or have you forgotten about that already, forever,

buried it beneath the pines, like remnants of
a lost civilization somewhere in the mountains
of Oregon or Northern California? It's not too late
to go and find it, if only I hadn't wasted

so much time looking for that lost map
and trying to explain just what it was that first
made me start out on this journey to other shores
where the sand is truly whiter

than what we have here at home in our backyard.
What can I do if all of my explanations
fall on deaf ears—stop explaining? Let them
figure it out for themselves?

Now in mid-morning, church bells are ringing
and sunlight is streaming down into this room,
contradicting the long-range forecast
with a symphony of light and leaves.

Romantic Ruins

As the train was leaving the station
and the sun was setting on rooftops
of new-fallen snow, I began

to miss you and the lights went on
amid the boat slips. The shining sea
was China blue and I thought of you.

So what else is new! There are factories
that come down to the edge of the water,
a bridge that spans the horizon

while beneath it newspapers blow in the wind,
snapping against a wire fence. Parts of cars
are beginning to rust and an easy chair,

not even worth the attention of someone
with an eye for what is old but still useful,
has begun to lose its insides

like an unattended scarecrow in the country.
What is this thing called romance?
No, not language, but love.

Still it is a type of language we call
home, which is where you hang your
holidays out in the breeze or take them

to the cleaners, though not too often because
the good doctors say too much is enough
of this or that, yet there is a time for

too much of a good thing, like that maroon towel
you draped around your shoulders
returning from your bath last night and

out the window and over the bay that bridge
keeps on rising above me as its lights
reflect on the mirrored surface of the water.

A Dream of Ties

for Gerrit Henry

Red ones, of all shades,
brocade, wanting to trade some
with you for each of our birthdays.
Oh, those Geminis. Ties of many colors.

Mine are in my suitcase; yours
are on the bed, draped over your pillow,
streaming down like crêpe-paper
streamers onto your white sheets.

"That's very handsome. I'll take that."
And you do, but somehow I can't
get over the feeling that it's
the one you gave me

for my birthday last year.
"Here are some more," I say,
and you like this one and that
one too. Now it's my turn.

But yours are all silk, I say
to myself. Perhaps I better only
take one. That one, so blue
and red with a gold lace inset,

will do and I do. Still,
before leaving I want to have
the one you gave me last year back.
The desire lingers and then fades

as the sounds of our voices
mingle with street sounds
coming from outside
your window.

Tires hum across hot pavement.
A large truck pulls up and
backs into a parking spot.
That bird continues to sing in a tree.

Bridge Traffic

There's nobody I serve
who hasn't crossed my threshold,
even that French sky surfer
everyone is talking about nowadays.
You know what he says,
"Life is short, play hard."

You mean it's a holiday and
you're not sleeping the afternoon away,
but writing your first piano compositions:
"One Finger,"
"Don't Go Away,"
"London Bridge Flower," and
"London Bridge Ball."

So you try not to be
anything less
than what you are.

When all is said and done
I too may not have to take advantage
of that offer for free panic disorder treatment.

No use going on a wild-goose chase
for the happy means to financial independence
when it's right there in front of me,
like the song of the night

played on a Spanish guitar,
or that April morning
when I looked out the window
and saw, beyond the sheer white curtains,
the tangled boughs of trees
and a sky of dusky rose,
just above the ridge.

A Coat of Many Colors

for Joseph

When light shimmers on the water

like the morning sun on your eyes,
is that a hint of paradise?

Above the tops of tall trees
with their flowerlike leaves,

the big yellow sign says it well
—there is a sun in Sunoco,

a city design in the country fabric,
as in father and son, you and me,

and your mother gathers light from your eyes
like a harvest moon in an evening sky

in this bountiful season,
your first autumn on earth.

Money in the Streets

It's not a small town, or an old town.
It just sprang up amid the pines near the ocean.
On Saturday night, they cruise the strip,
hoping not to be resequenced, since
there is light at the end of the tunnel, but
you can stop your car and play musical drivers
before you reach a comfortable cruising altitude.

Along that same line, her hair is naturally wavy.
Were you able to find a time when you had
a few moments to yourself to unfold the sheets
before the rains came to wash it all away
down that wide avenue into the gutter
pushed on by winds of enormous forces and
followed up with a gentle breeze from the west?

Once upon a time, in a restaurant by the sea, a sailor
said to me, "You can't change boats in mid-stream."
And I've always remembered that evening
when the sun set over the city, illuminating
the twenty-two miles of hotels and motels and coffee shops
which line the beach. The wet sand glistens
with orange streaks, but now half the pier
has disappeared and the whole town is in the process
of restoring itself to its former glory, that plateau
before the storm. High above the street,
the chimes in an old church tower ring

while below sea gulls hover over two lovers
walking side by side with food in their hands.

"It's getting so bad," she said, "that you can't even
go out at night. It didn't used to be like that
when I was younger." And it was then that
the storm struck, tearing up walkways which reached
down to the water's edge and pools with views of the ocean
or hidden behind tall wooden fences
put up in a day so lovers could sunbathe nude,
and that was just the beginning of it all.
It got much worse before it got much better.

Who am I to say when or where it will all end?
I have my hopes and my desires, but why
are they any more or less important than those of others?
Could we call upon you to represent us
in high places or must we depend on the one
you choose to voice our fears and cares?
Eventually, the best route will reveal itself
and none of us will feel left out. Even
the slightest touch of your hand sends shivers
up his back and now there is the six-o'clock news
which must somehow make up for that short time
he used to spend with the evening paper before dinner.

Croton Reservoir

The receiver is off the hook and hanging
a foot above the ground

The mouthpiece is broken open and all its cords
are pulled out

There is a streak of light above the ridge
over the dark reservoir

This *is* the beginning—space for rent,
someone fitting the above description

He also was sent packing, so there's nothing
like crossing that bridge when you come to it

In the end, it all turned out the same as it would've anyway,
even if you had done something differently

Who's to know, a body of water for public use and
he wouldn't talk to anybody about anything

He called it minding your own business,
customized learning and insulting

with a broad range of fine poverties
Such was earthly life

The bagpipes have been playing
all morning long and into the early afternoon

The clock has struck the hour of noon,
the hour of the Angelus

Now you can see the pink haze on the hillside,
and shadows in the open forest

River Legend

They thought they could see it by boat,
but it was not in service at that time,

on this side or on the other side of the river. Still
it was a pleasure just to breathe in the hyacinth air around her.

He was not very good at fantasy golf, but
could deal with people on an individual

or personal basis. "I was just kidding," she said,
thinking of an old home movie

full of symmetrical clutter. When her grandparents
moved back here from out west, she already

had a family of her own and her son
was beginning to take his first steps alone.

Every morning he waited for the first sign of light
before he got up to make her coffee.

Making ends meet was harder back then,
so no one ever complained about not having enough

because there was always very little to go around
and everyone had to share what they had with others.

One day his luck turned and changed all that.
There was more than enough of what was needed,

though luxuries were still reserved for special occasions.
She held her hands together when she walked toward him.

He welcomed her with open arms. They were like
newborn kittens chasing after a ball of yarn.

That was twenty-five years ago, and now he still
likes to fish and hunt, and she needs a week

to rest up from vacation. Down by the river
an old band is playing a Civil War tune

while ladies in white dresses wave their fans at the tepid
summer evening air, in a town like Zanesville, Ohio, perhaps.

She smells like a flower and you like an old spruce tree.
All along the riverbank white driftwood has washed up

onto the shore and the last glimmer of light in the sky
flickers on the calm surface of the water.

As the somber tones of the minister's hymn fade
into the foliage along the steep bank

the drumming beat of a Saturday night rock band
rises in the distance. "Where does this walkway

lead?" she asks. "This goes all the way up
to Riverside Park. Then you have to turn around

and come back," a stranger replies.
She turns her head quickly and

shakes her long hair out of her eyes. His mouth
opens with utter amazement in the shape of a half-moon.

No Reservations

This is for you.
It's the best I have in the world.

That's the way I feel
every time I walk down
a Manhattan street in the twilight,
especially during the holiday season.
Still it's bump and go,
all the way to Penn Station,
at least until the conductor comes by saying,
"Woodside next, all tickets!"
But everybody has to make a living somehow
—a local car service,
the Gigi Bicycle Shop, Topaz Realty?
So no one has the right to assume
this is shady business.

It was so late at night already
I didn't feel like going anywhere special.
Next time we'll have to get some better bank financing
to improve our station in life.

And then the rain began to fall again
while we were watching the Korean channel,
clothes lying all over the place,
even on the incredible furniture.

Brief Chronicles

A spirit cannot linger, so what is that low haze
above the boats and the bay? We are preparing
for a tropical depression, something to talk about
tonight over dinner if all else fails.
What would you expect from lovers of extreme trivia?
They're members of an ancient guild
like the wine merchants of New York.

Someone said it was easy money.
It was just bad planning, but is there any other kind?
You sat there staring up at the apartment house lights
shining in the misty night,
thinking it was too late, it was all over
for you now. Why hadn't you started earlier,
instead of repeating that favorite phrase of yours?—
"No! No! A thousand times no!"

You were suddenly overwhelmed
by a feeling of complete futility,
and then she stepped down
off the streetcar at the corner
and walked by you in that long white cotton sweater,
holding a small envelope in her left hand
and a golden chain of keys in her right.
She was so close she could smell your cologne
—Copenhagen, or was it Chanel?

Your luck was in the cards,
in the simple knowledge
that we do what we want to do
when we want to do it—no earlier, no later—
no matter what anyone else says or does to us.

"Are we there, yet?"

"It's not far, now.
If you look up when we get to the top of the hill,
you'll see that small town
glimmering on the horizon below the starry sky."

Trouble in Paradise

Or is this Babylon again?
Are you out on a limb or can you stand up
now and be counted? The general

is almost rational when you're not around,
so keep a stiff upper lip and
walk into the mouth of the lion.

"Let's see if I have another dime
for this," he said as he fished
into his pocket and came up

with an original tellurian homily
on love. If only, at the drop of a hat,
you could return to that original time

and place where it all began
before the pens lost their caps and
Penelope began to unravel by night

what she had woven by day,
then, as if out of the clear blue sky
a lightning bolt had descended and struck

the earth only yards away from your feet,
you would begin to dream again
as you used to do when you were a small child

rocking in your mother's arms, but now
what you know is so much more,
or less, than what you knew then.

French Radio

Then he got into something, the whole truth
and nothing but the truth, and rumor was
it supported bird life. They say he's
on his way to a carnival in Rio,
but was there enough time before he hailed that taxi
to call someone who wanted to hear from him again?
The music has a way of getting louder,
when you are alone in the back seat.

Out in the kitchen I heard the smell
of coffee and the sound of cheerful voices
floating into the midnight-blue bedroom but neither of them
seemed to remember what had happened the night before.
In those days, there was hardly a crossword puzzle
        I couldn't solve,
but I'm to bed already, though the night is young.
There you are by the side of the road.
He sees you—can you see him?

This bus is now not in service.
That's grist for the mill. What is the last thing
he'll see on earth before his plane takes off?
A ruined wooden dock, slanting down into the water,
heaped with old tires and boxes, the broken sides of boats,
the moss-covered rocks along the eastern shore,
or the sun glistening on the water beneath a bridge?
His feet may touch down too on the fine white sand
        of the Sahara.

He talked a blue streak. It wasn't until then
they realized they both had something in common. "Hold onto
me," he said. "I'm not just a one-way ticket."
Those dahlia and canna bulbs were in the mudhouse
     all winter long
amid the leaves that rolled in whenever the wind blew.
Up on the ridge two pine trees drooped under the heavy snow
and a sliver of the moon formed the thinnest line I'd ever seen.
So it was night and all the stars lit up the dark sky.

He was standing underneath a streetlight beside a building
plastered with movie posters. A dark-haired guy
had just stepped out of the shower, but had forgotten
to pull down the shade in the bathroom.
There was a lamp in the bedroom window,
with barely enough light to read from before going to sleep.
A group of people by a car were all standing around
     looking at a map
as if they were lost. "Does anyone know where we are?"
     someone asked.

You walked out of the Velvet Cup into the cold night air.
There are so many things you don't know about him
and then you remember something he once said and you
believe in him again, climb the red
carpeted stairs, turn the key in the lock,
pick up the phone and call.
He turned up the collar of his coat
against the cool night air.

"I'll call you Jack." "Call me anything you want," he replied,
"but call me back." They were always on good terms.
It all started after the concert. Next there was
a Caribbean cruise and a week at the Acapulco Princess,
where they easily lost track of time. Then they were
both in Queens, living on spaghetti, macaroni,
and egg noodles. What use is there trying to pretend?
They were made for each other.

But I don't keep track of those things (that's their job),
though I hear they were neck and neck at quitting time.
Should he have bought you those fancy flowers?
There was no guarantee you would dress for dinner,
and so your routes diverged, a fork in the road,
and then he stopped at the National Grocery Store
where the sum total of his purchases left him
change for a phone call and a single taxi fare.

Paper Tigers

Now you appear to me when I least expect it,
caught in the web of sunlight that dawns beneath my eyelids
in the earliest morning hour or framed in the windowpane
on a cloudy gray morning while the yellow leaves
with their brittle brown edges move up and down in the wind.

If only you had been marooned on some desert island,
never to be heard of again, or sent back through centuries of time
to live the life of a beached seafarer on uninhabited shores
where the Atlantic crashes against the Cornwall coast,
but you are there in front of me and yet I cannot touch you.

Though your appearance is brief
like the shimmering light above a fragment of glass,
I know if my hand could extend beyond that surface
you would simultaneously step out of the frame
to take my hand in yours,

but every muscle in my shoulder is stretched to the limit
like the arm of an animated toy soldier and still I cannot
        touch you.
Do *you* know if we will be able to resist those great tides
that are pulling at the threads of our fingers,
threatening to toss us onto the moonlit sands?

The Big Screen

Smoke was rising from the abandoned dock
on the side of the bay. Not a single person was in sight,
though it was very unlikely anyone could have walked out
onto that marshy shore beside the railroad tracks.
In the time that it took the train to pass by,
the billowing smoke diminished and disappeared.
Later, two subway trains, almost the color of the seats
in the amphitheater of Shea Stadium,
crossed paths high on the elevated track
below a thin cloud of factory smoke
in the clear afternoon sky.

Was that the brick church
where we went for your father's funeral? We'll have to
pick up where we left off. Sometimes the world's
not as well-organized as I think it is. At other times
it runs like clockwork, but I'm not moving with it,
though that could be a blessing in disguise.

It was an unforgettable night in the woods,
not a star in the sky, but you shouldn't have
traveled all the way down there
just to see those palm trees swaying in the wind.

You were the one who taught him the joys of a bubble bath and
how to listen closely to songs on the radio.
He hasn't been the same since and still can't
get through an entire classical symphony.

Have you heard of Willie the Poet? I wish I hadn't,
but I should have given him the time of day
before the train left that evening.

When you called after the snowstorm, the entire room
was filled with the soft white light of the descending sun
and now every window in the house
is a shade of pink and blue.

Local Traffic Only

Turn toward me one more time
so I can see your face again
before you vanish down that street all alone.
The sky is deep pink
in the wake of a distant volcano's roar.
Even now I can hear your voice
and see your eyelids rise and fall
in the dim light of the café.

What directions do we follow,
what puzzles can we solve?
No one can know for sure, but
sometimes in the middle of a chapter of a novel
I think for a moment that I do.
Under the influence of a constellation
it all came true like that morning
when eleven geese crossed the road in front of us.

At first I didn't take the chocolates.
Later I wanted them
even more than I didn't want them before, but
there are many more important things
to think about in life
like the way you sometimes shake your shoulders
and lift your hair off your forehead
before you sit down next to me,
or the way your light is being spent

attending to all that unfinished business
out on the pier
near the Sea Breeze Restaurant.

Can we always recount our principal pleasures
or remember the exact amount of cash tendered
for the previous purchase?
When I pull back the shower curtain,
clouds of mist move out
into the cool air
like wind currents
off the Pacific Northwest coast
while beneath the bright city lights
a dark continent sleeps.

The Temples by the Sea

> *Why it was December then*
> *and the sun was on the sea*
> *by the temples we'd gone to see.*
> ~James Schuyler, "February"

They always seem as if they are about to vanish
but they don't. Sometimes they're here and
sometimes they're there, like that unexpected
reminder of the last days of summer
or the threads of a multicolored coat and that
symphony of sweet notes showering you with kisses
when you turn your face towards
someone who is just about to touch you.

Will your gold bracelet bring you home again or will
       your journey
end on some distant island where the only hope left to cherish
is the arrival of a ship bringing news of lost relatives?

The dew is on the grass again, but a nocturnal bird has filled
your sleep with its strident cries, and its black
       mottled feathers
cloak your eyes with the cloth of forgetfulness, honey
made from memory in the hollow of your mouth.

You are on the brink of a discovery which God,
with infinite wisdom, could not have made, and yet

your hair still falls forward onto your brow
when you toss and turn on the bed of snow beneath you.

A cloud casts a shadow over your awakening body
in the hour that even a grandfather clock could not strike, and
the darkening sky above the mantel is yet another sign
        of your dismay
at the way these temples have shaded
your half-erased portrait in the sand.

The Balconies of la rue Berri

for Gaëtan Racine

We've lived to see another spring, but you
are no longer with us, yet the memory of our
visit to your home on la rue Berri,
where life seemed almost eternal,
will always be with me, as will you
and the soft husky sound of your voice
pursuing a thought like a winding cobblestone street
in some little French village
or an avenue of Old Montréal.
Who could forget that or your balconies
overflowing with flowers, vegetables and fine herbs,
and those enormous overhanging sunflowers?

It's often in the early spring,
with the first warm days, after a long winter,
that you seem to be so near,
almost as if you had the power
to descend into the city in which I live
and walk down my street. Wasn't that
the sound of your voice again?
But where did it come from, as if in a dream?

Not too long ago
I lost someone else I loved,
and he kept returning to me in dreams

to say that he was still alive,
that I shouldn't live as if he were dead and gone.
In one of those dreams I saw him
in the hall of his building in Gramercy,
and I said, "You are still alive," and then
when I woke up, I kept thinking that he was alive,
that I had to call him. In my first dream about him
it was a very stormy night. I was on a wooden bench
waiting for a bus, when the pay phone
nearest to me began to ring.
I picked it up so it would stop ringing
and he was speaking to me.
When I asked him where he was, he said
he was nearby on the outskirts of the city
and that he would see me soon.

So maybe you too are nearby, but what puzzles me most
is whether or not you can now see the things I do.
Often I think you can and I suddenly get embarrassed
and start to think, "Oh, my gosh,
I wouldn't be doing this or saying this
if you were in the room," but then I think about it
          for awhile and
realize that if you are here, perhaps you only know
vaguely how I am behaving, but even that
changes the way I act, since I wouldn't want
you to think terrible things about me for time immemorial.
There are so many things I know I wouldn't do
if I knew you were watching me with those
light-blue movie-star eyes of yours.

Flights of Angels

for Ned Hoopes

Out the window and across the street,
The leafy boughs of trees are moving up and down
In the wind, but have you made the needed preparations
For your journey to the eternal city?

The bobbing tops of poplars that have grown above
The railing on the bridge's exit ramp
Bend to the breaking point in the gusts of rain
Descending from a radiant late-afternoon sky.

Rows of office windows rise above the ramp
While fluorescent lights glow like street lamps
Over commuters who will pour out into the wet air
When that invisible clock strikes the happy hour.

There is a question in your tears which sounds
The deep chord we try to hide from others, yet sometimes
The very depth of feeling while walking down a city street
Can chill you to the bone.

One side seems to continue where the other side
Leaves off and the way up is the way down unless
You're in the attic, or in the end
Is the beginning—if there is an end.

Now it's raining in Central Park and much of metropolitan
      New York.
You fall asleep with the smell of eucalyptus leaves
And a familiar sound on the radio as something
      deep inside you
Rises above your body into the night sky.

In the Theater of Memory

for Maura O'Leary

On that somber morning
When the curtain fell
And the stage door opened
Onto a sky of leaves and golden sunlight,
You felt the earth shift on its axis
Like the changing of the guard
Or the end of one age
And the beginning of another.
But this wave does not begin or end.
It springs up on the sea's horizon
And moves toward you
Until it breaks, spreading
Its fan of foam on the beach,
And you are drawn deeper
Into the foliage
Toward the ones you are left with,
The survivors at the height of summer,
And a promise of rain.

Uncharted Waters

Lean down your face towards me for a moment
and let me caress your cheek or your lip
as we descend into the valley below.

Suspended above that thatched hut, these willows
weeping by the water are heads of curly hair
turning from side to side on a blue pillow.

Why is he walking along the tracks down by the river
with a lantern in each hand? Does it have something
to do with the dimness of the mid-afternoon sky?

Either too much or not enough, but the dead
comfort us when we are alone in the falling rain
like that tilted rowboat on the grassy shore.

The foliage is thicker now and old houses
look new again, so let's not forsake the lights
that lead down the tracks to our home.

It's dark when we go into the tunnel,
but the train emerges on the other side
in a shower of sun and shadow.

The seeds on the maples are red with longing to be green
and the motley tops of houses along the tracks
are as bright as the polish on your toes.

You can rest your feet on the seat for balance
though first you must take off your sandals and lean back.
Where are we now, Alice? Down the road a ways,

near the hazy mountains on the horizon?
There's white dogwood back in those hills and
the afternoon has begun to give way to evening.

"The light is beautiful at this time of day,
isn't it?" "Yes, yes, especially when the sun
filters through the leaves onto the highway

that twists from side to side in the distance."

Once in a Blue Moon

You are looking for something new and different
beneath the unfinished buildings of this towering city.
You recite the litany of your private history to yourself,
hoping to find a key that will unlock the mystery for you
or some forgotten detail that will help you
put all the pieces of the puzzle back together again,
once and for all, but the rain keeps falling,
trickling down into the gutter, making its way
toward that larger body of water down below.

Maybe we suffer because we naturally fall away from
rather than out of love. This time it will be easier,
you will get it right, someone will understand you
and not take off in a completely opposite direction
only to be hauled back again to the starting point
where what was intended and what was understood
began to diverge. If just this once, someone could
ask a question simple enough to be answered clearly, then
you might emerge from the chaos that threatens to engulf you
each time you venture out onto the vague sea that
        surrounds you.

You are not waiting on the edge of this romantic chasm
for the sun to go down. It will follow you
through the bare autumn trees. On the far side of the valley,
icicles cling to the rocks and pines push their way up
out of the trees rising to the horizon.

Sunlight has broken through the cloud bank
and chased the patchy fog away,
playing tag with the letter of the law.

Even though everything is not perfect here,
you can be glad about the big things that go right
rather than sad about the little things that don't.
Slowly but surely, little by little,
trust begins to fill the spaces
left open by your uncertainties,
like water finding its way along the rock,
breaking over the ledge that separates the stream
into columns. The light is golden now
in the tops of white birch, gray oak and evergreens.

Released on Your Own Recognizance

The light you see on the other side of those trees
is the sun on the water. You are living through
one of those chaotic times
your father warned you about, but soon
its logic will seem much clearer to you
than you ever thought possible.
The most difficult thing is to decide
what to do now, since whatever it is
will have an influence on how it will all turn out.

You are off to a running start, hoping
that this time you are playing with a full deck
and not just toying with that perverse wish
to make a hole in the water. After all the waiting
your board has ended up on top of the surf
with you standing on it and there's nothing you can do
except ride it out and enjoy it as much as you can
before the view is lost forever.

You could take a photograph of it
just to remember how it really was,
but you prefer your memory of it
to the one caught in the lens
of the camera you bought for your Alaskan vacation,
the one you decided to take on the spur of the moment
just to win a bet you had made
with a fellow office worker

who never imagined you would be foolish enough
to pick up the gauntlet he had thrown down in front of you
        one day.
Oh, those were the days! And as the clock struck five,
you wandered out alone to your car
for the long drive north.

The Enigmatic Horizon

Is it possible that you can leave this all
to chance or does some decision have to be made
at some crucial point in the future, which will
change the course of your plans, if you have any, that is?
It is, sometimes, as if you had experienced this
            all in a dream,
or in several separate dreams and are now living through it
            again
and meeting the same people you met before, or thought
you had met before, but you must have met at least
            one of them
because his face is so familiar it couldn't have been
just a face in a dream—yes, that one with the chiseled cheeks
and that private-eye holster strapped over his shoulder.

So you are reluctant to live your reality
which seems to have been forced upon you,
or did you choose it with an eye on the future
knowing you would have to make a choice somewhere
            along the line?
Still it wakes you up in the middle of the night
like the light of the moon breaking through your window
and onto your bed, seeping into the farthest corners
of that luscious darkness where you felt safe and secure,
alone and away from whatever it is you somehow cannot
bring yourself to make an effort to understand.

Maybe you don't have to, but isn't it asking
too much to expect a reply? For if there were,
all the greatest fears imaginable might surface
and congregate on your temple where the pulse
of a gentle finger could do as much as all the tea in China
to quiet that longing to know, to get an answer now,
once and for all, even if now is never today nor certainly
       tomorrow.
This is merely a life you want to live and yet perhaps
you could live it and that is what tears away at your
surface of calm, that vinyl you have on the cover
       of your notebook
which someone gave you as a gift, not for better or for worse
but just until the blizzard stops beating at the door
       of your home
in the narrow street down there where all the windows
burn with an amber light into the early morning hours.

Not Just Anywhere

Snow is on the hills and trees that surround
this little town lost in sleep and dream. The low sun
is burning in the black silhouettes of branches.
A stillness hangs over the sloping ridges, but it seems
as if at any moment a strange forgotten sound
like the eerie cry of a myna bird in some faraway tavern
might emerge from beneath that fir tree which candidly
links the earth to the sky.

The glowing windows of a three-story house
welcome the approaching mist rising out of a distant
valley. Is there also a music suspended
over the smooth snow-packed surface of the yard
or has it already reached the traffic lights
that shine in the cold winter evening
like beacons frozen in time?

I am not sure where you are going. Rivers sometimes
flow with the tide, but there is no river in this town
so you cannot walk into it at the same place twice,
even if you once thought you could. Perhaps you
        will stop here,
though I don't know why you should bother; all the buildings
are tilted and the streets go up and down.
But you don't have to pump your own petrol
at the station which sells "Major Brand Gas."

Way out along the highway, other house lights
glitter in the wake of the silent air,
but you don't have to worry about them now.
They will be there tomorrow night
unless the rain washes them away,
taking with it the calm countryside
over which my eyes have so often wandered
on my way home from another town
that some say resembles this one,
though you certainly don't agree
or you wouldn't have lingered so long at the diner
over your navy bean soup and coffee.
The waitress, in her black dress and white-lace
apron and cap, has begun to wonder
if you are ever going to leave.

But don't let me deter you from the course you have chosen
to take. It's only a rare and fleeting moment you are looking for
and you might find it somewhere along the road behind you
or the one that stretches out in front of you,
cutting across the new-fallen snow
like the trail of a cross-country caravan
that passed this way long before you arrived.

On the Erie-Lackawanna

for Wolfgang Bernard Fleischmann

Great circles cross in the night,
but during the day they are straight lines again.
There is no explanation for all of this.

I must simply accept it as part and parcel
of the package you received one morning
just after you had awakened.

Yet there is very little reason to worry.
You are safe now on the other shore, and

I have stepped down from the stairs
of the train and placed my feet
firmly on the ground again.

A Full Seven Days

Seven days of golf, seven
days of tennis, seven days
for the price of six . . .
What's that you say,
"there's nothing good,
but something bad comes of it?"
I thought it was the other way
round. It's an ill wind that
blows nobody good. Is it six of one
and half a dozen of the other, or six
to one and half a dozen to the other?
Thank God we had the heat on
till the fuse blew, or was it
the electricity that went out?

It was like a blanket
over the entire island,
a dark cloud opening
in the sunny vista.
Someone said the guy tried
to pull the wool over my eyes,
but I've always known
that when it comes to business
there's more than meets the eye.
I've got to have my own take
on the way things work,

or someone will just come in
and tear the whole place apart.

There goes my phone again.
I'm going to answer it,
against my better judgment: "Yes,
I think he probably does . . . Oh,
you mean tomorrow . . . Well,
'fasten your seat belts,
it's going to be a bumpy night.'"

Twilight Bar

The water has reached the innermost recess of the bay
where whitecaps lap the sandy beach, and now
I can remember your face again, half in sunlight
and then again in shadow. In the azure sky,
the paths of two rockets and an airplane
cross above a metal globe, near the site
of what was once a World's Fair, and that bridge
looks like somebody's idea of a holiday decoration.

Once she said to her friend that he is not a big doer,
that he prays to a statue of the Virgin
in an old upright bathtub in his yard, thinking
now and then of his final resting place
in the Resurrection Rest Home beside the tracks.
Even now he can remember how he wanted
to stare at her for a very long time, but knew it would be
unacceptable behavior. Yet that first glance
might have been worth more
than a whole night at the Hollywood Motel.
Maybe that skier, with the word SKIMAN on his vanity plates,
is headed there right now in his red Camaro.
Thanks to computer imaging,
he may already be imagining himself out on the slope.

That little village used to be a resort community,
a place to go to get your body moving again.
"Do you know who my witness is tomorrow?"

"I have no idea, but I'm sure by now he's off the menu."
"It's Monday, anyway, so basically, it doesn't matter
whether he wants to do it or not."
"So then there's no point in me telling you my opinion."

Just send it out along the dog-barking chain,
and hope that someone will pass it on—
tree bark, a boat, a night of walking along the park.
If I hadn't stepped on that woman's foot in the train,
I'd feel better now about everything else I have done today.

"What you need to do is take care of yourself," he said.
Sure, we all need a little time for ourselves, to think about
the teeming waves of modern life, erupting on the shores
of our living rooms night after night
on the colored TV sets that gallop from news
to game show to late-night news again, but
what you see is who you are.
Or is it what you do?

All news is old news, but some of it may be necessary.
How can you avoid it? It's all around you,
even when you are quietly sitting
on the top of a building in Woodside, Queens,
soaking in a few morning rays
before returning to your desk and
your easy-loading Swingline stapler,
that trusty tool of everyday life,
from which a logical escape

might be a Southeast Asia tour. We won't pay extra;
it's cheaper to go on our own. But then we'll have the problem
of where to sleep for the night.

From this window in Manhattan, I can see two bridges
going in different directions—one north and south,
one east and west, and the elliptical rays of sun
bounce off the windows, off the windshields and chrome
of cars that pass each other like ships in the afternoon night.
"It's the eclipse," he says, "a dark light,
like the end of the world
or the beginning of another."

Mediterranean Sands

I imagine you in the full sunlight of September.
The white sailboats with their empty masts
rise and fall
in the undulating water of the harbor.
Small buildings dot the horizon
and a silky sand
leads to the water's edge.
I did dream about you last night,
but you were doing something I've never
seen you do before.

Now you are naked, lying alone on the beach,
in the scorching heat that surrounds your body.
I don't usually think of you this way
but somehow today the way the sun
falls down onto the concrete sidewalk
reminds me of your body next to mine.

I left all my notes
about how much I love you
in a book I was reading. You are probably
too beautiful for words,
though I might be able
to begin to describe you
if I were lying on a bed by a window
watching the sun on the sea.

Perfect Weather

Can't anybody say it's a nice day
and put $100 bills in my pocket?
"Billy," he wrote, "bring your folder out
so we can write notes, OK?" The crumpled piece of paper
rolls down the street carrying a message
one boy wrote to another at school.

In the distance, white light
and lamplight, oak leaves and
poplar trees. A train winds its way
through the valley while cars flow
down the avenue. A truck
breaks at the corner and moves on
southward through the intersection.

"So then, she goes to the therapist and when
she gets there, closed." Another day in the dark.
The distant sound of a low-flying plane
drifts into my bedroom and wakes me.

The bay opens northward, mist rises from
the water. There's a gingerbread house
beside the tracks down by the station.

Big yellow leaves and crimson sumac
signal the arrival of winter—
time to turn on the heat,

close the windows, try to make the short days
last a little longer, cuddle up next to you
and warm up the bed, and stay that way
holding on, a few hours,
all night long, forever
to remember your love.

Jellyfish Beach

Perhaps I can find words to suppress my gratitude
to you. "I'm sorry guys, but this is not
the gold mine that you thought it was.
In a land of lace curtains and old navy clothing,
let service be your guide. Go premium
in this world and the next, but don't count
on finding a skilled sailor in your boat
every day of the week." If you
forget to turn on the meter and someone
pays you, then what do you do with the money?
Keep it, of course, but beware the thought patrol.
If your imagination has run wild, you might have to
go out on horseback and bring it home again.

Paradisal passage through the humid air. "So you had
a good trip?" "Yes, three days on land and three days by boat."
Sunlight layering the leaves, making them lighter
or darker and strips of illumination streaking the ground,
lighting our way through the forest and into the trees.

Oh no! There's the rain I hoped wouldn't fall so hard.
It pours down onto the windy beach, running
in ringlets around and around the sculptures in the sand.
"Please don't give in to that incubus you described to me.
What can I do to help you expel it from your body?"
It rises like a wave of mania and then subsides.

Your cries still echo in my ears, calling out to me
as if from the pitch blackness of your near despair.

If only your body was free again to walk
this strange new earth. Why did you turn away from me
just when I most wanted to see your face? Today
you have begun to watch me more closely, to
eavesdrop on my conversation, to appear in signs
on storefronts around town. I imagine you are
looking at me as I am about to cross a street,
your hair flying in the breeze, your back
now against that window. Do you want to
make sure that I arrive safely on the other side?

Icy days fell upon us when we were in the South Tyrol.
While the mountain air blew your hair across your forehead
and you lifted your face to savor the cool breeze,
I wanted to take you in my arms and press you against
        my chest
to feel the warmth of your body.

This is the place of our everyday life.
We continue toward each other
to the point of no return: you and me
—our love, our work, here together and now.

Free Storage

Someone left it here long ago and now
it is buried too deep to ever find again.
A friend of mine once told me
that if I am really in tune
I will receive from that great wheel going around
the being which my being in tune has allowed
me to take from it and
bring into the world at that time.

Morning falls softly onto the threshold
of every building in the sunny city.
I can smell the fresh sweet rolls
baking in the kitchen of The Steak Shop,
when all of a sudden
up jumps the joker's assistant to tell me
that anything I say
can and will be used against me,
that he who laughs last
laughs best.

At the elevator, a sign
says, "Press up or down button to call car,"
but that is easier said than done.

We tramped slowly over the new leaf fall,
watching the sun's slanted rays
shine through the bare limbs of trees.

This is the house where our hats live
between seasons, and our lawn mower
is the motor of the city.

Golden Pages

The calm water of the bay
glistens in the late winter evening.
So it's come to this: the question
is evidently about new money.
She doesn't have to steal the man she wants
from the arms of another woman.
And behind her still
are silence and the pines.

So that's where they've been putting
all that snow they removed from our city streets.
The tow trucks are out,
even this late at night.
How can a truck that size
go down a street that small?

She's seen those backyards
many times before, but never
with that much ice and snow.
She's spent half her life in a hammock
on a sandy beach by the ocean, dreaming
about a hotel like an Aztec tower,
with gilded windows in the setting sun.

A popular culture is not a town without a name.
Remember the time he complained
about having sex in the woods?

That bothered him the most. It
doesn't make that much difference now,
but he could have written her
a letter explaining why.
It's still not too late, but for what?
If only she were alone with him now
by the fireside in that city by the sea.

Lights on the Sound

Our story begins on a dark and stormy night
or once upon a time, in a faraway land:
"Ladies and gentlemen, the fresh snow is very slippery.
Please be careful when departing the train."

I've always been subject to these silly romantic ideas
which are not to be trusted, but if you want to go
looking for some swingtime Cinderella, just because
every eligible maid will be there, you can count me out.
All the evidence suggests I have some substantial ideas
to defend, the way the moonlight
illuminates the bottoms of the distant clouds, perhaps?

This afternoon, there's a new blanket of snow on the old
woodpile, but it hasn't been used all winter long, and I am
so cold I want to sit here forever by the table in the kitchen
and let this afternoon sun coming through the back window
sink deep into my skin, warming me to the very center
of my bones. There, it seems, an old slow-burning
fire is about to go out. All I am thinking about is
whether the sun will reach those hot coals
in time to add just a little more fuel to the fire.

What also troubles me is not knowing what hurdles
I will have to cross to better understand
the desires of my neighbor. Who knows?

He may be the greatest surgeon in the world
Or even a mechanical genius.

One night in the rain or snow is not enough
to give us anything to go on. We'll have to
follow the clue left by his nephew's son,
the one who used to cut the lawn
before growing up and going away to college.

He was a one-size-fits-all shopper, but that was
merely a hobby; no one knew what he really did for a living.
Yesterday she was here, and today she's gone.
She's on her way. And when you ask the little pilot
where the plane is going, he always says, "To Paris, France,"
or "That's not a very good question."
So whatever reason you had for asking
will have to be thoroughly examined
before we can get to the bottom of this.
Maybe she is so beautiful
she has begun to get under his skin.

Once, a long time ago, I heard a rumor
that in his youth he spent every summer
with friends out on the Island,
but often when I say "the Island," someone asks
"Which island?" "Staten Island? Long Island?"
And I start to wonder how it's possible to communicate at all
when what we usually are doing is merely

talking in a vacuum and it's only the miracle
of human contingency that allows us
to occasionally glimpse from afar
what anyone else is ever saying or thinking, yet
little problems can grow into big problems
when you say things you don't mean.

Last night after the lights were out, I began to dream
about an old house with a hidden room
where I could take a shower. Then in the early morning hours,
I would say it was around 2 a.m., I awoke very suddenly
and couldn't get back to sleep for quite awhile.
Just as I was falling asleep again, you woke up
and couldn't get back to sleep either. It was like
the changing of the guard at the palace, a vigil maybe,
for a lost friend or loved one. I have a feeling
we will never be able to explain why this happened,
      but maybe
you're right when you say it has something to do
      with a problem
you are processing the whole night through,
even while you think you are sleeping soundly.

I also don't know why I spend so much time
thinking about what I am going to do rather than
doing it. Well, it's never too late
to change, but it won't do much good
to look for more savings and values when I can't afford
what I'm looking for in the first place.

Everybody seems to be tightening the belt these days,
even tighter than before, though the new administration
was supposed to bring a change in consumer spending.
It always amazes me that what goes on
at the highest levels of any bureaucracy
has nothing at all to do with what one needs in one's own life,
especially if you have very little money to begin with.

They must have been doing that all winter long, but
the last few mornings I have noticed
the lingering smell of wood smoke
coming from a neighbor's fireplace. What
a good idea to heat up the house that way
in the early morning after waking.
I suppose you thought you could get out of town
without saying goodbye, but there you are again,
bumped off the last train out of here
because you didn't have a reservation.
Are these the turns and twists of fate,
or the way back to the garden of Eden,
that shopping mall on the side of the expressway?
If that's where you're going, it's always better
to take the service road, especially in rush hour traffic.

This morning the sky was overcast and gray,
but soon after I lifted the shade
a swatch of sun broke through,
brightening the shuttered windows
of the house down the block.

A couple of sea gulls,
with glittering wings,
twisted and turned in the sunlight
before it dimmed and disappeared.
The whole day was business as usual
in what is often referred to as a tough economic climate,
but that night when I closed the office
and walked downstairs to the car,
the last streak of sun had stuck there on the western horizon,
casting a glow on the water
and above it, the lights of the bridge
burned like streetlamps in the twilight sky and
reflected on the smooth surface of the Sound. Oh, what
a few caresses wouldn't do to make your bright eyes shine.
All I need now and then is a little attention too,
just to know someone cares. We often end up
in the same place but not in the same shape. I was there
under the covers, even as you stretched your arms
to pull off your sweater when entering the room.
The next day we returned to the same café
but I didn't realize until we had driven away
that I had forgotten to pay for our already discounted lunch.

A Safe Harbor

I've seen her change clothes in a taxi
and it was amazing. I mean not her body,
which is beautiful, but the way she changed her clothes,
though I guess a taxi is as good a place as any.
I had a friend in college
who used to carry a toothbrush around with him
if he knew he wouldn't be
waking up the next morning in his own bed.
One gets so busy these days,
the hectic pace of modern life and all that.
I often wonder what happened to him, and what
he could have meant by his favorite saying,
"Here today, gone tomorrow."

What was it like in that bedroom?
There where all the preparations were made.
Was it that they lost sight of their goal for awhile
or did one of them just stop believing in the other?
Maybe it was more than that. The result
couldn't have been much worse,
a kind of human sacrifice, but for what?
That too may be clear to us some day.

This morning she began to dig in the flower garden again,
her bare hands touching the earth
to give that flower life. He wanted to touch
the curve of her neck. What other question

could he have asked of this bronze face
turned upward to the sun?
Someone said that clichés
were on sale. Probably for a dime a dozen.
What is it that allows some people to see the value
in what others have thrown away?

No one wants to say the sky is falling,
because it isn't, yet.   But then
why is the emperor buying new clothes?
What I've seen there does not indicate in any way
whether or not he can do the job. We'll
simply have to take our chances and hire him
on the spot or we'll lose yet another
of the treasures that has crossed our threshold
and entered the golden door. Could it be
that we are still only dealing
with the tip of the iceberg?

"Why Me?": A Fantasy for You

In her dream
she is lured
to a plush velvet couch
in the lounge
of a local body shop
by an irresistible
garage mechanic.
"Well, and what are
you two up to? . . ."

Don't go away!
Our feature movie will resume
after these brief messages
from our sponsors.

If this is a commercial break,
it's time for a little comfort food.
There's never anything to eat
in this cold-water flat. But did you
see the way those two looked at each other?
That was either a long look or
a short brush fire.

I'll just leave you
with these happy thoughts.
What use is it
to keep her whereabouts a secret?

She can't hide hair of sunshine gold.
For the first time in a year
he will sleep well tonight.

Modern Screen

People used to take the night boat to Albany
for entertainment, or it was off to Tuxedo World,
followed by a visit to The Jefferson Democratic Club.
"Oh look, honey," he said, "old Betsy is just about
to reach 100,000 miles. We'll have to record this for posterity."

The trouble nowadays is you can't get enough
available airtime, with so many
other people using their cellular phones.
We should all be so lucky or is this just another way
to clutter up the information highway to the moon.

I'm either a dog of few barks or a man of many words.
Sometimes you need to have a little irony
about your feelings. Of course, one of your greatest admirers
is not a genius who's been teetering on the brink
of the void for much of his adult life.

People will do anything these days for a laugh,
even pull down their pants in public, though that's
no laughing matter. Often I think of you way
off there on the other side of the world and wonder
if my letter will ever reach its final destination.

If I hadn't been such an impossible person, you wouldn't have
to sleep so far away, but my view of these things
is a little warped, now that I've read all those books

you suggested I read before taking my next step into
the twenty-first century, never knowing when the storm
          will break.

All along the skyway people come and go without
realizing that they've seen one of the great wonders
of the universe in the valley below. Down there, workers
swarm like buzzing bees going about their business
while intrepid postmen refuse to let sleeping angels lie.

Photo by Raimundo Mora

About the Author

Eugene Richie is the author of a poetry chapbook entitled *Moiré* and a co-translator of *My Night with Federico García Lorca* by Jaime Manrique (also from Painted Leaf Press). His poems and translations have appeared in publications such as *The Denver Quarterly*, *Poetry New York*, *Mudfish*, *Private: Arts*, *Ploughshares*, *The Literary Review*, *Broadway* II, and the *Anthology of Contemporary Latin American Poetry*: 1960–1984. He is a founding editor of The Groundwater Press and teaches at Pace University in New York City.

This book was printed in April 1998 by BookCrafters, Chelsea, Michigan, for Painted Leaf Press. The text is set in 11.5 point Novarese Medium and is printed on acid-free paper.